KEEPING
THE
MAIN
THING

To Fielden Sanders,
Thanks for preaching
for me this past Sunday,
and thanks for all that
you do for West End
United Methodist Church
God bless you! Amen
                    Rich Lindamood

Feb. 5, 2020

TIMOTHY C. TENNENT

KEEPING THE MAIN THING

A NEVER-CHANGING GOSPEL IN AN EVER-CHANGING WORLD

 Seedbed

Unless otherwise indicated, Scripture quotations are taken from the Holy Bible, New
International Version', NIV'. Copyright © 1973, 1978, 1984 by Biblica, Inc.™ Used
by permission of Zondervan. All rights reserved worldwide. www.zondervan.com

Scripture quotations marked ESV are taken from the ESV® Bible (The Holy
Bible, English Standard Version®), copyright © 2001 by Crossway, a publishing
ministry of Good News Publishers. Used by permission. All rights reserved.

Scripture quotations marked KJV are taken from the Holy
Bible, King James Version (public domain).

Scripture quotations marked RSV are taken from the Revised Standard
Version of the Bible, copyright © 1946, 1952, and 1971 the Division of
Christian Education of the National Council of the Churches of Christ in
the United States of America. Used by permission. All rights reserved.

Printed in the United States of America

Cover design by Strange Last Name
Page design by PerfecType, Nashville, Tennessee

Tennent, Timothy C.
    Keeping the main thing : a never-changing gospel in an ever-changing world /
Timothy C. Tennent. – Franklin, Tennessee : Seedbed Publishing, ©2018.

    pages ; cm

    Includes bibliographical references
    ISBN 9781628245745 (pbk. : alk. paper)
    ISBN 9781628245752 (mobipocket ebk.)
    ISBN 9781628245769 (epub ebk.)
    ISBN 9781628245776 (updf ebk.)

    1. Jesus Christ--Messiahship--Meditations. 2. Jesus Christ--
Lordship--Mediations. 3. Redemption--Christianity--Meditations. 4.
Messiah--Prophecies--Meditations. 5. Christian life--Methodist authors--
Mediations. I. Title.

BT230.T46 2018   232/.1   2018963763

SEEDBED PUBLISHING
Franklin, Tennessee
seedbed.com

In loving memory of Jean Marie Daughtrey Myers
(January 1, 1928–January 21, 2018)
My mother-in-law, the one who showed us all the
way of love in Jesus Christ.

Contents

Introduction

Do you remember the film *Saving Mr. Banks*? It was about the background to the making of the famous film *Mary Poppins*. The film brings us into the inside struggle between P. L. Travers, the author of the book *Mary Poppins*, and Walt Disney over the rights to turn the book into a full-fledged film starring Julie Andrews and Dick Van Dyke. In some ways, it is a classic tale of contextualization. How do you preserve the original message of the book while presenting it in a different format to a different generation? This is the "form and function" tension. Can Dick Van Dyke dancing between several animated penguins (a major point of contention between Travers and Disney) help preserve and communicate the book's message for many generations, or does it cheapen and trivialize the message so that the substance of the book is lost? The book is about saving Mr. Banks. The film obscured that point quite a bit and ended rather weakly with Mr. Banks going out to fly a kite.

I couldn't help watching the film from the perspective of the challenge we face as communicators of the gospel. On the one hand, the gospel message does not change. Jesus Christ was crucified on a cross and raised from the dead to deliver condemned sinners like you and me. That basic message does not change. On the other hand, entering many churches today feels more like walking into a Starbucks or Panera Bread than entering a hushed sanctuary or an exalted cathedral. Pastors are sometimes asked to communicate their message between a bunch of dancing penguins. Of course, we shouldn't forget that going to church in the first century was neither a Starbucks nor a cathedral-type experience. Both of those expressions are highly contextualized for their respective times. I am not one of those who stand against various moves to contextualize the gospel, though I have been critical of some aspects of the contemporary church. I have also spent many years as a professor of missions, teaching about the need for contextualization of the gospel.

Yet, we must always be cautious when, in the name of contextualization, the substance of the gospel is forgotten or lost. I would never raise serious concerns about someone who put the Apostles' Creed or prayers of repentance to a contemporary tune. But I have wondered why a church would drop the Apostles' Creed or prayers of repentance because they are not seeker sensitive. I'm fine with dancing penguins on either side of Dick Van Dyke. The moment the film is no longer about saving Mr. Banks, but about how to fly a kite, then I think we need to step back and reevaluate if we have forgotten the whole purpose of contextualization. In the same way, we must rejoice and embrace all kinds of creative ways of bringing the gospel to a new generation. In the process, though, we must not lose sight of the central message.

This book is a collection of meditations on various passages of Scripture from both the Old and New Testaments. Each passage has been carefully chosen to follow the great redemptive thread of the Bible, which points us to Jesus Christ. The three Old Testament passages demonstrate the expectations and longings for the Messiah that Christ fulfills. The next three passages focus on the ministry of Jesus, culminating in His crucifixion and resurrection. The last two passages help us to see more about how the church lives out the gospel under His lordship. In every case, each chapter is designed to reinforce or point to the central message of the Christian faith. The centrality of Christ is a message we must not neglect.

∽ One ∼

Songs of Hope

1 Samuel 2:1–10 and Luke 1:46–55

Several years ago, someone submitted a newly
released Christian book to be reviewed. The reviewer
wrote the following shocking and yet memorable
words about the book: "A truly Christian book must
contain three elements: color, fire, and music. Since
this book contains neither color, nor fire, nor music,
I must conclude that it is not even a Christian book."
It was, of course, a devastating review. But it does
point to a great insight about what happens when
true Christianity touches anything, be it a person's

life, a church, or even a book—it gives it color, fire, and music.

The two passages of Scripture we are meditating on are filled with color, fire, and music in many profound ways. These texts are normally used in the church during the season of Advent, when the church tries to recapture what the world was like before the Messiah first came into the world, as well as our own hope as we look for His glorious second coming at the climax of the ages.

The two Scripture texts are songs sung at the two ends of the great prophetic stream. The Old Testament passage, from the lips of Hannah, is the first and earliest messianic song of expectation. The New Testament text, from the lips of Mary, is the final and culminating song at the point of fulfillment. Both songs pour forth from women, each at the end of the prophetic history of her age.

We should envision this great stream of the prophets as a long rope that stretches from the dawn of prophetic expectation to the high noon of prophetic fulfillment. Along that rope lie all the great prophetic hopes, dreams, longings, and expectations. The rope stretches out over a thousand years. The prophet Isaiah is on that rope as he foretells the coming of Immanuel and the One called "Wonderful Counselor, Mighty God, Everlasting Father, Prince of Peace" (Isa. 7:14; 9:6). The prophet Jeremiah is on that great rope as he foretells the coming of the "righteous Branch" who will bring us a "new covenant" (Jer. 23:5; 31:31). The prophet Ezekiel is on that rope as he foretells the coming of the servant shepherd (Ezekiel 34). Daniel is on that rope as well. He looks for a "son of man," who will be given dominion and glory and a kingdom, and whom all peoples, nations, and languages will worship (Dan. 7:13–14). And on and on it goes, all through the Old Testament, each prophet anticipating the coming of the Messiah. Each had his own insights into the true majesty of the Messiah. But the entire rope is being held on either end by two young women, Hannah and Mary. They are the ones God chose to hold the two ends of the rope.

Song of Hannah

We begin by looking back at the first song, the Song of Hannah. Hannah was a young Jewish woman who lived at a time of great spiritual darkness. First Samuel 3:1 says that "the word of the LORD was rare" in her day. It was a tough time. Hope was in short supply. Yet, out of the darkness came color, fire, and music—the first messianic song in the Bible— pouring forth from the heart of Hannah. It was from her barren womb that the first Old Testament prophet was born, Samuel. The name Samuel means "God heard." What did God hear? God heard the Song of Hannah. In response to her messianic cry, God set into motion the people and events that would finally culminate in the incarnation of Jesus Christ through the womb of Mary. We still sing about this great story. In the famous Christmas hymn "Hark! the Herald Angels Sing," Charles Wesley gave us these words:

> Veiled in flesh the Godhead see,
> Hail th' incarnate Deity!

> Pleased as man with men to dwell,
> Jesus our Immanuel.

Yes, the songs still go on, but Hannah's was the first. The Song of Hannah is about hope. Hope is believing in something that hasn't happened yet. It is about what can happen with small beginnings and sincere prayers. Hannah was in despair over her barren womb. Bearing children has always been a sign of fruitfulness and the blessing of God. Hannah was barren. Her own barrenness seemed to reflect the spiritual barrenness that was all around her. Eli, the priest of Shiloh, was so spiritually barren that he interpreted Hannah's agonizing prayers, not as earnest petitions, but as the babbling of someone intoxicated with alcohol (1 Sam. 1:13). Eli's sons, who represented the future of the priesthood, are described as wicked. The Bible openly acknowledges that they "had no regard for the LORD" (1 Sam. 2:12). In short, there were no prophets. There was no word from the Lord. The priesthood had become corrupt. The whole history of redemption hung on the prayers of Hannah. She was holding the end of the rope. We

9

all should thank God that Hannah didn't let go of the rope. She prayed. Hannah's Song anticipates great things happening in the world, not through human strength, not through human ingenuity, not through human power, but through God's anointed one. She looked to the day when a messiah would come. This is the first time the word "messiah," the Hebrew word for *anoint*, is used in the Bible. Hannah was inspired to see that the hope of the world was not in priestly "anointing," but in a Person, an "Anointed One." She turned the whole focus of the prophetic stream from looking to ritual acts to looking for a Person. The word "messiah" means "the Anointed One." This is the same word translated in Greek as "the Christ."

Hannah envisioned the day when the Messiah would bring about a great reversal. In 1 Samuel 2:4 she sang, "The bows of the warriors are broken, but those who stumbled are armed with strength." In verse 5 she envisioned a day when "those who were full hire themselves out for food, but those who were hungry, hunger no more." It is a picture of God coming to judge the world, and setting things right. Even in her own barrenness she had the faith to declare, "She who was barren has borne seven children, but she who has had many sons pines away." Hannah longed for the day when the Messiah would come and interrupt the endless flow of evil and wickedness in the world and assert His rightful claim on the peoples of the earth.

For Hannah, the universe was not the result of some chance collision of molecules, nor was the world's social status shaped by mindless economic forces. History is not the product of mere dialectical materialism or sociocultural evolution. Behind all human history stands the God of the universe, who is sovereign. It is to Him that Hannah directed her amazing prayer. She held on to the rope when no one else had the courage to think like this or pray like this. Hannah's Song is filled with declarations that make God the subject: The Lord brings death and makes alive (v. 6). The Lord sends (v. 7). The Lord raises up (v. 8). The Lord guards His people (v. 9). He thunders from heaven. He judges. He gives strength (v. 10). Finally, it is the Lord who sends His Anointed One (v. 10).

For Hannah, God takes orders from no one. He was created by no one. He remembers nothing because He has forgotten nothing. He learns nothing because there is nothing He does not know. He does not need to recall because He holds all truth simultaneously. He is the God of the eternal now. Every point in history is eternally present to Him. He can look at human history from the beginning or the end or the middle, for all things are known to Him. And He stood by a young Jewish girl one day and inspired her to utter something in hope and in expectation that at the time seemed impossible. She dared to believe that with God all things are possible.

No one realized that Hannah was holding the end of a prophetic rope that would someday lead to the incarnation, a rope that would be fully realized on that great day when men and women from every tribe, nation, and tongue will shout, "Hallelujah! For our Lord God Almighty reigns," and "The kingdom of the world has become the kingdom of our Lord and of his Messiah, and he will reign for ever and ever" (Rev. 19:6; 11:15).

The priest who witnessed Hannah's prayer thought she was drunk. He couldn't hear the song. But God heard the song. Out of the faltering lips of a young Jewish woman came pouring forth the good news of God's Messiah, the Anointed One. Hannah dared to believe that if God could turn the barrenness of her womb into the fruitfulness of a little boy named Samuel, then He can turn the barrenness of our ugly sinful world into the fruitfulness of God's visitation. Hannah articulated at the very beginning of the prophetic stream what would happen when the Messiah stepped into the world. Against all odds, she held on to her end of the rope and sang her song.

The Song of Mary

The same God who heard Hannah's prayer stood at the other end of that stream with another young

Jewish woman, named Mary. Hannah's prophecy is known to the church simply as Hannah's Song. Mary's Song is known as the *Magnificat*. It is one of the most ancient Christian hymns, since it is recorded in the New Testament and appears in the very first chapter of Luke's gospel (1:46–55). Mary's Song begins, as does Hannah's, with an act of worship: "My soul glorifies the Lord and my spirit rejoices in God my Savior" (vv. 46–47). "All generations will call me blessed," she declares (v. 48). Mary is blessed not only because she has been chosen to bear the Messiah, but also because she was chosen to hold the other end of this great prophetic rope. She will be blessed because she will be on the right side of this great reversal that Hannah first spoke of more than one thousand years earlier. Mary goes on to articulate the great reversal with language that is very similar to Hannah's: "[God] has performed mighty deeds with his arm; he has scattered those who are proud" (v. 51). "He has brought down rulers from their thrones but has lifted up the humble" (v. 52).

"He has filled the hungry with good things but has sent the rich away empty" (v. 53).

Mary's humble estate was mirrored by Jesus Christ Himself, who came not to Plato's Academy, nor to Herod's Palace. He did not even come into the world in the Jewish temple. Rather, He came to us in a lowly stable, born as a Jew, born under oppression, soon to be a refugee. Who would have believed that this birth was the hope of the world? Yet, somehow, Hannah and Mary knew.

Mary knew that heaven would not turn on decisions made by US or Chinese presidents or by British or Indian prime ministers. History for Mary, as with Hannah, is directed by God on the throne! James Lowell captured this truth so well in his hymn "Once to Every Man and Nation." The hymn concludes:

> Though the cause of evil prosper; yet the truth
>   alone is strong;
> Though her portion be the scaffold, and upon the
>   throne be wrong;

> Yet, that scaffold sways the future, and behind the
>   dim unknown,
> Standeth God within the shadow, keeping watch
>   above his own.

Yes, the song continues to be sung, as we, too, anticipate the final climax of the ages, when Christ will return at the Second Advent and set all things right. We are now in a season of grace to gather as many as will come under God's rule and reign. But in God's own time, the curtain of history will someday fall, and we will all be called to give an account of our lives and hopes. Our lives should be filled with color, fire, and music as we join in with these two dear women of faith. We, too, must put our hands on the rope and lay claim to this great message that is for the whole world. We must join in that great song which Jesus Himself is singing. It is a song filled with color, fire, and music.

Blessed to Be a Blessing

Psalm 67 and Psalm 87

One of the iconic symbols of American pop culture was *Star Trek*, which gave us James T. Kirk and the most famous extraterrestrial, the Vulcan Spock. It was Spock who made famous that Vulcan greeting and blessing with upraised arm and split fingers: "Live long and prosper." What is less known is where that hand gesture and greeting came from. You may be surprised to know that Spock's famous Vulcan greeting was derived from the same source that gave us this anointed prayer in Psalm 67.

Leonard Nimoy, the actor who played Spock, was the son of Ukrainian immigrants. He grew up in Boston, Massachusetts, in a home of strict Ukrainian Orthodox Jews. As a young boy growing up in an Orthodox Jewish synagogue, he was fascinated by the blessing that the priest would give from beneath a prayer shawl, with hands lifted and spread in the very manner that would later be used by Nimoy's popular character, Spock. The split fingers that make up the priestly blessing mimic the Hebrew letter *v*, which begins the famous Aaronic blessing found in Numbers 6:24–26:

> "The LORD bless you and keep you; the LORD make his face to shine upon you and be gracious to you; the LORD turn his face toward you and give you peace."

It is probably the most famous blessing in the entire Bible. Only the sons of Aaron the high priest were allowed to pronounce it. Today, Jewish priests never say, "Amen," and they change the name *Yahweh* to *Lord* during this blessing because only a direct descendent of Aaron can pray this prayer and say the covenantal name of God. It is a sacred prayer in which God's covenant name is used three times:

> YAHWEH . . . bless you and keep you
> YAHWEH make His face to shine upon you . . .
> YAHWEH lift up His countenance upon you.

In the Hebrew, the prayer is beautifully planned, with each verse slightly longer than the one before it: three words, five words, and seven words, symbolic of the ever-expanding blessing of those who live under God's covenant. The priest, the son of Aaron, pronounced the blessing in the temple in Jerusalem, with his hands upraised over the people, fingers split in the same way that centuries later young Leonard Nimoy would observe and import into popular culture.

Psalm 67 is a seven-verse prayer and act of worship from ancient Israel. This prayer cannot be properly understood unless you remember that it begins by recalling the Aaronic blessing. The psalm begins:

May God be gracious to us and bless us and make his face shine on us—[*Selah*]

It is the whole Aaronic blessing in seed form. It recalled for Israel, as it does for us, that we live as those under the blessing of God. Then—almost mid-sentence—a little, marginal word appears in the Hebrew: *Selah*. No one knows for certain what *Selah* means, but our best understanding is that this was some kind of pause or musical interlude to allow the worshipper to stop and reflect. We, too, should pause and reflect on all of God's blessings in our lives. As Christians, we are a blessed people. God has brought us up out of the bondage of sin. He has given us the righteousness of Christ, and He has blessed us with every spiritual blessing. He has also provided for our daily needs and watched over us in times of trouble. In short, to use the words of this psalm, God has blessed you and kept you. His face has shined upon you. He has lifted up His countenance upon you, and He has granted you His peace.

The genius of Psalm 67 is not just that it takes the Aaronic blessing and turns it into an act of worship, though that alone would have made it one of the great hymns in the Jewish Psalter. But what it does is far more profound than that. Psalm 67 bring two great truths together from early Jewish history. First, with the Aaronic blessing, it demonstrates God's gracious love for us and His covenantal promise to bless us. But then, it recites an even more famous Old Testament passage: the original covenant with Abraham, found in Genesis 12, on which the entire Jewish experience is built. It also begins as a blessing:

> "Go from your country, your people and your father's household and go to the land I will show you. I will make you into a great nation and I will bless you; I will make your name great, and you will be a blessing. I will bless those who bless you, and whoever curses you I will curse; and all peoples on earth will be blessed through you." (vv. 1–3)

This is the real inspired beauty of Psalm 67. It brings together as an act of worship the Aaronic benediction with the covenant of Abraham, which promises to bless all nations, "that your ways may be known on earth, your salvation among all nations" (v. 2). The most oft-repeated phrase of the Abrahamic covenant throughout the Bible is, "in your seed all nations will be blessed."

The Abrahamic covenant was God's answer to the confusion of the Tower of Babel in the previous chapter. The Babel account (Genesis 11) tells us three things about the inhabitants of the earth. First, they wanted to settle down. Second, they wanted to build a city with a tower that reached to the sky. Finally, they wanted to make their name great. This is the basic instinct of all of us apart from the gospel. We want to put down roots, build a monument to our own greatness, and make a name for ourselves. However, this is the very trap that can keep us from discovering God's deeper purposes in our lives. It is somewhat ironic that Genesis 11 is where we discover the bankruptcy of the world's agenda. In our own culture, "Chapter 11" is that part of the tax code that sets forth the terms of bankruptcy.

There is, of course, nothing wrong with building our lives and seeking to do well in this world. That is not the point. God does bless us in many tangible ways. The point is that the reason God blesses us is so that we might be a blessing to others. He blesses us so that others will come to know Him through our lives. Psalm 67 captures all of this in an act of praise, so we would sing about it, pray it, and live into it.

Is your life focused on being a witness for Jesus Christ and using whatever gifts He has given you for His glory? Elton Trueblood, the twentieth-century Quaker scholar, wrote in *The Incendiary Fellowship*:

> The only evidence that something is on fire is the pragmatic evidence that other fires are started by it. A fire that does not spread must eventually go out. A person who claims to have a religious experience, yet makes no effort to share and to extend it, has not really entered

into Christ's company at all. In short, an un-evangelistic or un-missionary Christianity is a contradiction in terms.[1]

In other words, we have been blessed to be a blessing.

Another writer, theologian Abraham Kuyper, once said, "There is not one square inch of the entire creation about which Jesus does not cry out, 'This is mine! This belongs to me!'"[2] He not only looks at the United States, Canada, and the United Kingdom and cries out, "This belongs to Me!" But He says this about Cuba, North Korea, Vietnam, Libya, India, Tunisia, Afghanistan, Cambodia, Iraq, Iran, Sudan, Uruguay, and Bolivia. The whole earth belongs to Him. He is calling forth worshippers from every tribe and tongue. He is calling forth worshippers from

---

1. Elton Trueblood, *The Best of Elton Trueblood: An Anthology*, ed. James R. Newby (Nashville, TN: Impact Books, 1979), 31.

2. Abraham Kuyper, *Near unto God*, ed. James C. Schaap (Grand Rapids: CRC Publications, 1997), 7.

all the earth. The praise of Jesus must be go forth in Mandarin, Farsi, Kurdish, Afrikaans, Lao, Dari, Hausa, Arabic, and thousands of other languages, to the praise of His glorious grace.

God does not just call a few people into ordained ministry, and the rest remain uncalled. All of us are called to be a part of this ever-spreading blessing. We become co-laborers with Him. The gospel must spread like a flame until it reaches the rice farmer in Tianjin, China; the textile worker in Hanoi, Vietnam; the literature professor in São Paulo, Brazil; the soccer mom in Seattle, Washington; the businessman in Budapest, Hungary; the information technology professional in Bombay, India; as well as the school-teachers in your city. Every inch of society and of this entire world is intended to be among the recipients of God's blessings. Amazingly, God does not just do this work and allow us to watch it. He calls us to be the agents through whom He blesses the world.

This same theme is found in Psalm 87, which may strike a first-time reader as an odd psalm. Why would an entire psalm be dedicated to people from various forgotten nations, such as Rahab (a poetic name for Egypt), Babylon, Philistia, Tyre, and Cush? Furthermore, why would they be found boasting that they were "born in Zion" (vv. 4, 5, 6)? We must understand that these nations represent the enemies of Israel. This is dramatic and shocking! To declare that Rahab, Babylon, Philistia, Tyre, and Cush will have the same covenantal claims as a Zion-born Jew is revolutionary. These verses simultaneously remember God's promise to Abraham to bless "all peoples on earth" (Gen. 12:3) and anticipate Christ's command for us to go to all the nations (Matt. 28:18–20). It is an early declaration that God's global purposes will someday include "every nation, tribe, people and language" (Rev. 7:9), as foreshadowed on the day of Pentecost (Acts 2:5–12).

At one stroke the seven verses of Psalm 87 demolish the widely held notion that the Old Testament is only about Israel, or that the people of God in those days had a very narrow, parochial view of God's wider redemptive purposes and we must patiently wait for the New Testament to show us God's deeper plan. God's global purpose is revealed from the beginning of the covenant in Genesis 12:3 when He promises to bless all nations. In Psalm 67, Zion is symbolic of what it means to be counted among those embraced by the covenantal, redemptive love of God! He is the fountain of life for all nations and all people. This is why Jesus, when He cleansed the temple of the money changers who had occupied the court of the Gentiles, declared, "My house will be called a house of prayer for all nations" (Mark 11:17). This is why we can join in this psalm and sing with all the nations of the world, "All my fountains are in you" (Ps. 87:7).

Take time to reflect on all the blessings in your life. Thank God and praise Him for these blessings. Then ask God to show you how you can be a blessing. In the end, our greatest work might not even be anything we do, but all the ways we enable others to do. The most wonderful thing about being a part of this great plan of God is that He has already given us a glimpse of how all these blessings will culminate in the end of time:

> Every knee [shall] bow . . . and every tongue confess that Jesus Christ is Lord, to the glory of God the Father. (Phil. 2:10–11 ESV)

Three

Righteousness Is a He, Not an It

Habakkuk 2:1–4

We actually know less about Habakkuk than we do about any other prophet in the Old Testament. He is widely believed to have been a Levitical singer in the temple, called to a prophetic ministry. Jewish rabbinical tradition claims that Habakkuk was the famous son of the Shunammite woman whom Elisha raised to life in 2 Kings 4. But we actually know very little about this prophet, as his name never appears in any other canonical writing. However, we do know quite a bit about the context in which he prophesied. It is not about us as pastors or teachers or prophets, but about our faithfully bearing the message in the midst of the times we are in. That, in itself, is an important lesson about ministry.

Habakkuk wrote in the midst of great anguish just before the Babylonian invasion and the exile of God's people. The claim that Habakkuk was a Levitical singer is significant because the book of Habakkuk is a lot like an extended psalm that unfolds over three chapters, consisting of a predictable complaint, the voice of God speaking, and a final, powerful resolution in 3:17–19.

Habakkuk lived under the crushing power of Babylon. He probably experienced the Babylonian campaign against Jerusalem, because in chapter 1, Habakkuk seems to be well acquainted with Babylonian cruelty (see vv. 12–17). He saw the final occupation and exile on the horizon, and he wanted to make sense of the whole thing as a man in covenant with God. The book is really, at its root, a complaint against God for His inaction against the Babylonians.

Indeed, he openly questioned why God would allow a nation so wicked—indeed, more wicked than Judah itself—to execute judgment against Judah. As chapter 2 opens, Habakkuk is waiting on an answer from God. It was this text, quoted by the apostle Paul in Romans 1:17, that became so transformative for Martin Luther at the dawn of the Protestant Reformation.

Habakkuk's Posture of Waiting

In Habakkuk 2, we see the prophet stationing himself in a tower to stand at his watch and to wait for God's response in the midst of unfolding tragedy. Before we move on to the divine response, it is critical that we pause to reflect on this vital posture of waiting.

We, like Habakkuk, are witnessing breathtaking evil that can crush our spirits and tempt us as a nation to abandon our faith in God. Each new day brings more news of instability, the advance of violence, the utter brokenness of our political institutions, the rapid decay of morality, the assault on the Christian view of the body and the family, the tragic loss of truth, and the diminishment of the meaning of words. The church's response to our time has been mixed. Some churches have gone into a cultural retreat, withdrawing from the world and giving way to criticism or despair. This results in a loss of our missional engagement and our love for a broken world. Other churches, particularly the mainline denominations, want to win the world's favor through boundless cultural accommodation. Thus, the church becomes nothing more than an echo chamber of popular culture rather than a prophetic witness to the saving work of the triune God in the midst of a depraved and lost generation.

Throughout this invasion of evil of Babylonian proportions, we are not accustomed to the long wait for answers from God, so perhaps Habakkuk might offer divine insight into a better way ahead. In the posture of waiting, we realize just how much we want God to play the short game, with easy solutions and quick resolutions. But God plays the long game. He calls us to be patient in the midst of our own calamities and remember that we are called to a life of hope in God's faithfulness. The Lord told Habakkuk to write the vision down and make it plain on tablets, for the vision awaited its appointed time—this is a theology of hope in the long game. If it seems slow, the Lord went on, wait for it; it will surely come; it will not delay (Hab. 2:3). The "revelation" of verse 4 is not the whole vision. Habakkuk only gives us the broad thesis of it with a beautiful couplet that contrasts the Babylonians with the posture of God's people.

Habakkuk 2:4 begins, "Behold his soul is puffed up; it is not upright within him" (ESV). This is the summary of the Babylonians. Whether the singular "his soul" refers to the Babylonian nation as a whole or to the king of Babylon—or both—it demonstrates that God is fully aware of the posture of those who stand in opposition to His rule and reign. In time, the Babylonian nation would be no more, though the spirit of the Babylonians continues in every generation—proud, arrogant, and certain of their victory. But there is a counternarrative found in the second phrase in verse 4: "but the just shall live by . . . faith" (KJV). This is the phrase that resonates through the new covenant and is quoted three times in the New Testament.

The Just Shall Live by Faith

Take a moment and reflect on this powerful little phrase: "The just shall live by . . . faith."[3] This is the seed of the gospel of Jesus Christ. I want to examine this phrase as it is quoted in Romans, Galatians, and Hebrews, because each of these texts brings insight into what it means to align ourselves with the purposes of God.

---

3. There are multiple alternative translations of this phrase, including "The righteous shall live by his faith" or the "Righteousness shall live by their faithfulness," and so on. I am stating it in the classic form "The just shall live by faith" (KJV) as it was traditionally phrased by the Reformers.

Romans 1:16–17

The first quotation of Habakkuk 2:4 is found in Romans 1:17. This phrase became the spark for the Reformation, which moved Luther beyond merely complaining about abuses in the church to the recognition and rediscovery of the gospel itself.

When Martin Luther was in seminary, at the University of Erfurt, the most influential theologians he studied were Gabriel Biel, Duns Scotus, Peter Lombard, and Thomas Aquinas. All the theologians of his day understood words such as *grace*, *faith*, *justice*, and *justification* within a framework of works and law. *Righteousness* referred to God's active righteousness, which enabled Him to judge us righteously. The phrase "the just shall live by faith"— especially in Latin—seemed to imply that we must become righteous if we are to have our faith accredited by God. Since God is holy and we are not, this, for a pre-Reformation Luther, was bad news—in fact, he said that reading this passage in Romans 1 was like "a thunderbolt in my heart." It was a constant reminder of God's righteous condemnation of sinners. But since he was trained in Greek, Luther decided to start from the beginning and read the New Testament in the original language.

One day, Luther was reading the book of Romans in his little study in the tower of the Black Cloister in Wittenberg, when he came to verses 16 and 17. There the apostle Paul says, "I am not ashamed of the gospel, because it is the power of God that brings salvation to everyone who believes: first to the Jew, then to the Gentile. For in the gospel the righteousness of God is revealed—a righteousness that is by faith from first to last, just as it is written: 'the righteous will live by faith.'" Luther realized for the first time, reading this in the original language, that Paul was actually talking about God's righteousness being *given* to us through faith in Jesus Christ. It was an alien righteousness—it was not one we had to earn, but one that comes to us as a gift from God through faith. This is the gospel. God is righteous and we are not; righteousness comes to us not through the works of the law, but through faith in the work of Jesus Christ. When Luther realized this, he said he "felt as if [he] was altogether born again and had entered paradise itself through open gates."[4] Romans 1:17, quoting Habakkuk, gives us the kernel of the gospel itself.

Galatians 3:11–14

Habakkuk is quoted again in Galatians. It was from Galatians that Luther learned to distinguish between the righteousness of the law and the righteousness that comes through faith in Jesus Christ. In Galatians 3:11, Paul wrote, "Clearly no one who relies on the law is justified before God," (there drawing upon the vision of Habakkuk). Paul went on, "Christ redeemed us from the curse of the law [that is, the path of earned righteousness] by becoming a curse for us" (Gal. 3:13). Christ took the

---

4. Luther's Works, vol. 34 (St. Louis: Concordia Publishing House, 1960), 336–37.

curse that was intended for us—and deserved by us! This is the gospel. But it is here in Galatians that Paul made the connection between Habakkuk's posture of waiting and the faith of Abraham, which was not in Romans 1:17. Looking back, Paul saw Abraham as the ultimate man of faith. Abraham was justified, not by his works, but by his trusting in God's provision. He learned to wait and to trust, and even though he never saw the fulfillment of God's promises, he remained steadfast in his faith.

Moses and the law were a necessary provision of God, but the covenant of faith *precedes* the law, going back to Abraham. This is why Abraham is the father of faith, whereas Moses is the Lawgiver. Abraham wouldn't see the promised land or the temple. The Babylonians would someday invade and destroy both. They would take Judah into exile. God's people would experience much calamity in the centuries to come, but the just shall live by faith! Luther saw that he had been stuck at Moses, reading all of Scripture through the lens of Moses and the law. Habakkuk 2:1, quoted in Galatians 3:11, helped him recognize the true antiquity of the covenant of faith and grace. "The just shall live by faith" goes back to Abraham, and the law was never meant to alter it. Through Paul's quote of Habakkuk, Luther realized that the Reformation was a rediscovery of the good news that was established from the beginning with Abraham and had been preached in the early church but had been lost.

Hebrews 10:36–37

The third and final quotation of Habakkuk is in Hebrews 10:36–37. The chapter begins with the posture of waiting. The author calls for our endurance. He remembered Habakkuk and the need to lean in to the posture of waiting. Then, the writer of Hebrews ingeniously drew a phrase from Isaiah 26:20 to personalize the vision. Remember: God had told Habakkuk that the vision was for an appointed time and to wait for it. Notice the word "it" in Habakkuk 2:3; it occurs six times in close succession:

"the vision awaits its appointed time; *it* hastens to the end—*it* will not lie. If *it* seems slow, wait for *it*; *it* will come; *it* will surely not delay . . . but the just shall live by faith. When Hebrews quotes this it says, "The *coming one* will come and [*he*] will not delay, but the [just shall live by faith]" (10:37–38 ESV, emphasis added). This final New Testament quotation of Habakkuk finally gives us the full vision. The righteousness of God is not merely an "it"; it is a "He." It is not simply that Christ gives us a *thing*—namely, His righteousness—but He gives us Himself. *He* is our righteousness (1 Cor. 1:30; 2 Cor. 5:21; Phil. 3:9).

In the gospel we finally see that God is not just giving us an alien, inanimate righteousness; He actually gives us His active righteousness in His Son. We are righteous because we are "in Christ." He is our righteousness. He is the vision that Habakkuk waited for. He is the city whose builder and maker is God, which Abraham longed to enter (Heb. 11:10). He is our peace. He is God's long game. God's plan is not a strategy; it is a Person. The Babylonians and all their spiritual heirs who fill the world to this day are finally defeated through Jesus Christ, who sits at the Father's right hand until all His enemies are put under His feet (Ps. 110:1). Death itself is defeated—not through something we have, but through the person and work of Jesus Christ, who is our Head and in whom we live and move and have our being (Col. 1:18; Acts 17:28).

In 2017 we celebrated the five hundredth anniversary of the Protestant Reformation. It was not an unwarranted disruption in the church. It was the recovery of the gospel itself, which is "Christ in you, the hope of glory" (Col. 1:27). The Reformation is nothing less than the rediscovery of the gospel. This is why we need a new reformation in our own day. Each new generation needs to rediscover the power of the gospel for a broken world. We don't have a plan to repair this broken world. We don't have a strategy to fix Washington, D.C. We don't have an evangelical blueprint to turn back the tide of moral chaos. We have something—Some*one*—much better: Jesus Christ, a crucified, risen Savior, who has borne the brokenness of this world and offers us all new hope through the gospel. The reason those six words in Habakkuk—"the just shall live by faith"—are so powerful is that they connect us to the whole redemptive vision of the Bible, reaching back to Abraham, the father of faith, who teaches us the posture of waiting. It reaches all the way across redemptive history to Jesus Christ Himself, the coming righteous One in whom all the promises of God find their fulfillment.

Righteousness is a "He," not an "it"—this is why Habakkuk came down from his tower of waiting, having heard from the living God, and concluded his prophecy by saying, "Though the fig tree does not bud, and there are no grapes on the vines, though the olive crop fails and the fields produce no food, thought there are no sheep in the pen and no cattle in the stalls, yet I will rejoice in the LORD, I will be joyful in God my Savior. The Sovereign LORD is my strength; he makes my feet like the feet of a deer; he enables me to tread on the heights" (Hab. 3:17–19).

Thanks be to God!

Four

God's Wounded Healers

Luke 10:25–37

The parable in Luke 10, which we call the parable of the good Samaritan, comes to us as an answer to a question: "Who is my neighbor?" It seems to echo in the New Testament several other powerful questions from the Old Testament that until now were left unanswered. When you read this question, you should hear, at least faintly, that famous question from the book of Genesis when, after Cain had murdered Abel and was confronted by the Lord, he asked, "Am I my brother's keeper?" (4:9). Perhaps you also recall the question that the Lord Himself posed in the book of Jonah, the only book in the entire Bible that ends with a question. The Lord asks, "Should I not have concern for the great city of Nineveh?" (4:11). Am I my brother's keeper? Should I not be concerned about that great city? Lord, who is my neighbor? These are all open questions that Jesus addressed in this same great parable.

I would like to draw your attention to this parable, but from a different angle. I want us to look at this parable, not from the perspective of the priest or the Levite or even the Samaritan, but from the underside: from the perspective of the wounded traveler lying in the ditch on the side of the road. Jesus said in Luke 10:30 that "a man was going down from Jerusalem to Jericho." This was a treacherous, seventeen-mile trip that descended three thousand feet from one city to the other. The road was filled with switchbacks and lonely, winding, hairpin turns with many rocks and boulders that seemed to invite robbers. A traveler would know it was a dangerous journey. Life can be dangerous. Indeed, Jesus went on to say that on his way to Jericho, the man "fell into the hands of robbers. They stripped him of his clothes, beat him and went away, leaving him half dead."

We are not told anything about this man. Jesus gave us no details—that itself is an important detail. We know neither his name nor his nationality. We don't know if he was married, single, divorced, or widowed. We are not even told why he was on this dangerous journey. We don't know if he was young or old, Jew or Gentile, rich or poor, believer or unbeliever. In modern-day terms, we don't know if he used Facebook or Instagram. It could have been you or me. The point is, he was on his way through life and he got wounded. Life can be a wounding experience, and it can happen to the best of us. It is a truism that life comes without any guarantees. This is why when we get married we say, "for better or for worse," because no one knows what life will bring our way. When you least expect it, you lose your job or you have a financial collapse. Perhaps you have gone through the pain of divorce or the death of a child. No one plans these things. They happen to the best of us.

But this is a parable about healing. God wants the wounded to be healed. And He wants us, as His people, to feel the pain and woundedness of those around us.

Notice carefully how the end of verse 30 characterizes this traveler: he was "half dead." Jesus did not say he was dead, but that he was half dead. That means that healing was still possible. This man was also likely in pain; had he been dead, he would have felt no pain. He was half dead . . . but he was also half alive.

If you're hurting right now in your life, God wants you to know that you are still alive! Healing is still possible. Now, if you stop feeling pain, either your own or that of others, then you're dead, spiritually dead, even if you're still walking around drawing a paycheck. Sadly, this world is full of walking dead men and women so caught up in their own pursuits that they no longer feel pain and no longer hear the cries of the wounded. There are people hurting all around us. They are the oppressed, the refugees, the hungry, the homeless, and most of all, those who have never even heard the name of Jesus.

Let's look at the travelers who passed by in this parable. The wounded man was lying there in the ditch—stripped, beaten, robbed, and half dead. It could have been you; it could have been me. And a priest passed by. The priest was a religious man, both respected and respectable. People called him "rabbi" and "teacher." He was probably on his way from Jerusalem to Jericho to conduct some religious meetings. The problem is that he got on a nonstop flight and couldn't take the time to feel the pain of those around him.

Luke 10:31 says, "he saw the man." The priest saw his wounds. He saw the blood. He heard the groans. But he passed by on the other side, fearing that he would be defiled as a Jewish priest. He felt no sorrow or pain because he had carefully insulated himself from the woundedness of the world. He was more concerned

47

with ceremonial purity than with practical piety, so he deliberately avoided any possibility of contact.

The same thing happened with the Levite in verse 32. He looked at the wounded traveler, but passed by on the other side. I submit to you that the man in the ditch may have been half dead, but this priest and this Levite were fully dead, even while they lived, because they felt no pain. Each was on a nonstop flight.

Some of us are on a nonstop flight up the promotion ladder. Or, perhaps, on a nonstop flight to retirement. We have so ordered our lives as to avoid the possibility of contact with pain and suffering. But we risk our own spiritual death in traveling down that path. *Just look at me; don't touch me*—that's the sin of the priest and the Levite. Their lives were only for show; neither could be bothered to respond to real human need.

Jesus was a man who touched and who could be touched. In the Gospels, we see Jesus constantly being interrupted. We see Him reaching out and touching lepers, sitting down and having meals with sinners, and never seeing these as a distraction but as the heart of His mission. Remember the day that Jesus was on His way to Jairus's daughter (Luke 8:40–56)? She was twelve years old and at the brink of death. In fact, by the time Jesus got there, she was dead. Ultimately, He raised her from the dead, but recall that on the way to Jairus's house to do ministry, something interrupted His plans: He got caught in a crowd.

This account is told just two chapters before the parable of the good Samaritan. It is no accident that Luke let us catch this contrasting glimpse of our Lord. Jesus was caught in the crowd, and there, in the midst of that great throng, we meet a wounded woman. We don't know anything about her either—except that she was wounded. She had an issue of blood and had been slowly hemorrhaging for twelve years. She had spent all her money on doctors who could not help her. In her desperation she thought, *If I can just touch the hem of Jesus' garment, I'll be healed.*

The woman made her way anonymously through the crowd, and she reached out and was just able to barely touch the hem of His garment as the throng pressed against Jesus. Jesus immediately stopped, turned around, and said, "Who touched me?" (v. 45).

Isn't this a remarkable question! Who touched Me? "Lord," Peter said, "what are You talking about? Look at the crowds of people who are pushing and shoving You." If you have ever been to an outdoor market in the Eastern world, or been to a major-league game, you know what it is like to be caught in a crowd. Yet, Jesus turned and asked, "Who touched me?" He said He had felt power go out of Him.

Jesus lived in a constant awareness of the needs and the woundedness of those around Him. Most of us are like Peter and the other disciples that day. For us, life is just a bunch of accidental contacts. We are so insensitive to the pain around us. But not Jesus. He was the most sensitive man who ever lived.

Those who heard Jesus tell the traveler's story the very first time were being cleverly set up. Jesus told them, "The priest passed by" and then, "The Levite passed by." His first-century hearers were probably smiling and nodding among themselves. *Yes, that is just like them*, they thought. How shocked they must have been as Jesus went on to say that a Samaritan was the only one who felt the wounded man's pain and stopped to minister to his needs. Samaritans were hated by Jews. They were marginalized as a mixed race, not fully Jews or Gentiles. But in Luke 10:33, we discover that it was the Samaritan who was compassionate, who wiped the blood away, carefully bound the victim's wounds, carried him to the nearest inn, and paid for his full care and recovery.

The Samaritan, you understand, was the least likely candidate to bring healing because he himself was wounded. He was familiar with rejection. Yet, he became a wounded healer, ministering out of his own pain. He reached out despite his own woundedness.

God is raising up wounded healers in the church today. He is raising up men and women who walk through the world in a different way. We go through life knowing that we have our own brokenness. We may have many questions as we face a wounded world, with crushing social problems and massive spiritual lostness. We ask, "Am I my brother's keeper?" We look out over our community and wonder, "Should I be concerned about this place?" We see people around us and ask, "Who is my neighbor?" These questions, and many more like them, are answered here in this passage, with powerful force.

This parable is a foreshadowing of the greatest Answer to these questions: Jesus is the ultimate Wounded Healer. He was wounded for our transgressions. He bore our pain and suffering. On the cross we see God incarnate. We see the one who stepped into the pages of human history, to walk amid our pain, to touch us in our woundedness, and to bear all our brokenness on the cross of Calvary. But now, as the risen Lord, He sends *us* out as His wounded healers, to hear and to heed the cries of pain and suffering. This is the way God is, and this is what we are called to through the gospel.

Five

Boasting Only in the Cross of Christ

Galatians 6:14–18

When was the last time you walked down the cereal aisle in your local grocery store? The choices can be overwhelming! There's Cap'n Crunch, Sugar Pops, Lucky Charms, Reese's Puffs, Cinnamon Toast Crunch, to name a few. Then there are all those "healthy" options, like Basic 4, All-Bran, Total, and Fiber One. Even if you choose Cheerios, you have to decide which kind of Cheerios: regular, multi-grain, honey nut, apple cinnamon, frosted, and so on.

We live in a very crowded world, with so many distractions. In some ways, going to church can be a bit like walking down the cereal aisle. We have to decide whether to attend the liturgical service, the traditional service, or the contemporary service. Most churches offer a wide variety of programs for children, youth, young married couples, older adults, and any number of other groups bound together by a common age, marital status, interest, weakness, or what have you. All of these can be good things, but it is important in the midst of a world filled with dizzying change and options to remember that which does not change, that which remains the symbol of every Christian sanctuary and, indeed, the heart of our faith: the cross of Jesus Christ. The cross can easily just blend in to the church architecture. More tragically, it can fade from our understanding of what lies at the heart of the Christian faith.

This is why Paul declared to the Galatian church, "May I never boast in anything except the cross of our Lord Jesus Christ, through which the world has been crucified to me, and I to the world" (Gal. 6:14). The Galatians, it seems, were being tempted—as we are today—to boast in other things. We boast about the beauty of our sanctuaries or the size of our congregations. We boast about the programs we offer or the good we are doing in the community. But Paul reminds us that the only thing we have to boast about is the cross of Jesus Christ. Why should we boast in the cross of Jesus Christ? Why is the symbol of the cross the centerpiece of our churches and our faith?

First, the cross is the place where we are transformed. It is there that we discover the true glory of God. We think of glory as the grand, majestic, awesome power of God. But this is a "hidden glory" that Jesus Christ revealed on the cross. His kingship was never more revealed than in His servanthood, which led Him to the cross. His authority was never more powerful than when He said, "No man takes my life; I lay it down of my own accord" (John 10:18). His power is never more evident than in the weakness and vulnerability of the cross.

The cross turned everything upside down. God redeemed the world not through a top-down display of force and power, but by entering into the suffering and pain of the world. The cross is not the picture of God's glory relinquished. It is the greatest expression of the glory of God! Only through the cross could God judge the entire world righteously for sin (Jesus bore our sins) and yet, in that very act, simultaneously offer His greatest act of mercy and grace to the world (Jesus offers grace and forgiveness to all who would trust in Him).

If the gospel teaches us anything, it is that God comes to us in unexpected ways. We see Him coming into the world not in a palace, but in a stable in Bethlehem. We see Him talking to a woman at the well, an outsider despised by her community. We see Him having a meal with Zacchaeus, a hated tax collector. We see Him in the presence of sinners and touching lepers. But, nothing could prepare us for God going to a cross so that we could have our sins forgiven and our lives transformed. The cross represents our greatest rejection of God. Yet, in the mystery of the gospel, our greatest rejection of God became His greatest embrace of us! Our greatest act of alienation became His greatest act of reconciliation! For "God was reconciling the world to himself in Christ, not counting men's sins against them," but nailing them to the cross (2 Cor. 5:19). Our worst act as a human race—nailing God to a cross, became His greatest act of grace—nailing our sins there. The cross represents our greatest "No" to God—saying, "God we don't want You in our lives, and we don't want You in our world." Yet, in the cross, we meet God's greatest "Yes!" to us. All of our "Nos" to God are swallowed up in the great "Yes!" of God in Jesus Christ! This is why the cross will always stand at the heart of the Christian faith. Even when the early church was being persecuted and had to meet in the catacombs, they scrawled crosses on the walls. Even then the church realized that the cross, which was in their day the most revolting sign of disgrace and torture, had been transformed into the greatest act of God's mercy and love.

Second, the cross is empty—reminding us that Jesus rose from the dead as the victor. The Roman Catholic church often depicts Jesus hanging on the cross. It is known as the crucifix. We Protestants do not reject that image, and in fact, some Protestant churches display the crucifix during Lent. However, early Protestants believed that another important lesson could be taught if the cross were displayed bare. It became a simultaneous pointer to the suffering of Christ *and* to His glorious resurrection. The cross points us not only to the price He paid, but to the victory He secured.

Paul wrote in Philippians, "I want to know Christ and the power of his resurrection" (3:10). This is why Paul boasted in the cross—it is no longer merely an instrument of torture or death. The cross represents Christ's victory *over* death. It represents His victory over sin and over every other lesser trial of life. It is therefore a symbol of God's power. The Scripture says that the same power that raised Christ from the dead is now being manifested in our mortal bodies (Rom. 8:11). The same power that emptied the cross is now available for us through the Holy Spirit working within each of us. Jesus holds the keys of death and hell! The stone the builders rejected has now become the cornerstone! The Lamb of God is the Lion of the tribe of Judah! (see Revelation 1:18; Matthew 21:42; John 1:29; Revelation 5:5).

This is why the church did not use as their central symbol either a stable or an empty tomb. The former would make sense as a symbol of the incarnation, another central teaching of the Christian faith. The latter would make sense because if Christ had not been raised, we would still be in our sins (1 Cor. 15:12–20). But the empty cross became the central symbol of Christianity because it gathers all these truths into a single emblem. If Christ had not become incarnate, He would never have suffered on the cross. If He had not been raised from the dead, the cross would not be displayed as empty. So, the cross has rightfully taken its place as the central symbol of our faith. We are the people of the risen Lord.

Third, the cross stands as God's victory over all the world's false religions and philosophies. Jesus said, "But I, when I am lifted up from the earth, will draw all men to myself" (John 12:32). This is a testimony to the global power of the cross to overcome all false ideas, shallow philosophies, and worldly wisdom. While every cross symbolizes this, I think it is probably best depicted in the Celtic cross, a cross superimposed over a circle. The circle has become a Christian symbol in, for example, wedding bands. But this is not the meaning of this ancient depiction that those early Christians found in what is today Great Britain. When these early Christians first arrived on the islands, Britain's occupants were practicing paganism—and the chief symbol of paganism was the circle, an ancient Druid symbol. Pagan beliefs and rituals had a very fierce grip on people groups throughout the British Isles. These are the ancestors of many who may be reading these devotionals—including myself. But the gospel triumphed over paganism, and the love of Christ prevailed!

As the lasting symbol of this great triumph, the Celtic cross was designed—the cross triumphant over paganism, and over every other false religion or lofty philosophy that stands opposed to God's revelation in Jesus Christ. In a proper Celtic cross, the cross should be displayed as superimposed over the circle, demonstrating the triumph of the gospel. I like this not only because it reinforces the earlier themes, but because here we do not have a simple, isolated cross—a cross detached from the world—but rather a cross that has engaged the world and emerged victorious. This reminds us that ultimately our mission is in the world. Paul said it was the cross "through which the world has been crucified to me, and I to the world" (Gal. 6:14). It was his way of summing up that great prayer of Jesus in John 17 when He prayed that we may be in the world, but not of it (see vv. 14–17). We are to be engaged fully in the world, but always with the triumph of Christ, which puts the world and all of its worldliness to death on the cross.

When my family lived in Scotland, we had the privilege of making a pilgrimage to Lindisfarne off the coast of Northumbria, one of the early centers of Celtic Christianity. There stands a moving statue of Aidan, the apostle to the English-speaking world, in front of a massive Celtic cross. The statue depicts Aidan looking out over the British Isles, holding in his right hand a shepherd's crook, showing the pastoral, nurturing side of the ministry; and in his left hand a flaming torch, emphasizing the light of the gospel and the ministry of evangelism. Just as those early Christians faced a world of paganism in a pre-Christian world and knew that Christ would be triumphant, today we face a new kind of paganism in our post-Christian world, and yet we know that Christ will be triumphant.

Let me conclude this chapter with a dramatic anonymous story about the great white throne of God, where the nations of the world will be judged. At the end of time, billions of people were scattered on a great plain before the judgment seat of Christ.

Most shrank back from the brilliant light of God's enthroned majesty. But some groups near the front talked heatedly—not with shame, but with belligerence. "How can God judge us? How can He possibly understand suffering?" shouted a young woman. She ripped off her sleeve to reveal a tattooed number from a Nazi concentration camp. "We endured terror, beating, torture, humiliation, and death." In another group a black man lowered his collar. "What about this?" he demanded, showing an ugly rope burn. "I was lynched, not for crime, but for the color of my skin." In another crowd, there was a young, pregnant teenager with downcast eyes who said, "Why should I suffer? It wasn't my fault and yet my parents rejected me."

Out across the plain there were hundreds of such groups. Each had a complaint against God for the evil and suffering He had permitted in His world. God had it easy, they concluded, living in heaven, where all was glory and light, with no crying or fear or hunger or hatred or war. What did God know about all the suffering that men and women were forced to endure in this world?

Each group sent forth its leader, chosen because he or she had suffered the most: a Hitler-era Jew, a black slave, a Hiroshima survivor, a youth who witnessed a school shooting. They presented their cases before God.

Before God could be their Judge, He must endure what they had endured, they said. They declared that God should be sentenced to live upon earth as a man. He must be born a Jew, in a system of apartheid, where He would live under oppression as a minority. The very legitimacy of His birth must be questioned. He must be given a job so difficult that even His own family would think Him out of His mind. Let Him be betrayed by His closest friends. Let Him face false charges, be tried by a prejudiced jury, and be convicted to die by a cowardly judge. Let Him be tortured, lonely, publicly shamed, and finally murdered.

As each leader announced his portion of the sentence, murmurs of approval went up from those assembled. But when the last had finished speaking, a great silence fell upon the masses. No one uttered a word. No one moved. For suddenly everyone realized that God, in His infinite love, had come and walked among us, and had been subjected to all of this and more.

This is the power of the cross. God entered into our world of suffering and pain. Yet, through the cross, He has brought salvation.

Praise be to God for the cross of Jesus Christ and His glorious resurrection!

Six

Finding Only Leaves

Mark 11:12–22

Philip Yancey, in his best-selling book *The Jesus I Never Knew*, chronicles his slow realization that the Jesus he had met in Sunday school was not the same Jesus he met in the pages of the New Testament. Yancey recalls a poster of Jesus that was displayed on the wall of his Sunday school class that portrayed Jesus serenely standing amid children in a pastoral setting, with a small, sleeping lamb in His arms. I vividly remember that very picture of Jesus, as it must have been displayed on the walls of Sunday schools across the country. The Jesus portrayed in Sunday school and children's sermons is often, Yancey commented, "a Mister Rogers before the age of children's television."[5] He was kind, gentle, reassuring, otherworldly, and most of all, very, very nice. However, at some point it dawned on him that no government in the world would execute Mister Rogers. It seems that the crucified and risen Jesus Christ of history continues to be a foolish scandal and a "stumbling block" to those who find their "nice" or "domesticated" Jesus contradicted by the vulnerability of the crucifixion, the boldness of His claims, or the divisive and prophetic figure portrayed by the actual eyewitnesses of His life and ministry, as recorded in the New Testament.

For years I squandered the season of Lent because I was so excited about the arrival of Easter. I did the same during Advent. The seasons of waiting, pain, and suffering are those windows in our lives when we can really learn and change and be transformed.

---

5. Philip Yancey, *The Jesus I Never Knew* (Grand Rapids: Zondervan, 1995), 13.

It's hard for us to really capture the plain fact that the first Good Friday was not known as Good Friday; only in retrospect can it be known as such. Sometimes we picture the disciples at the foot of the cross saying, "Friday's here, but Sunday is coming!" Yet, no one was saying to the soldiers, "Just give it three days, because He's going to rise again." No one who was actually at the foot of the cross said, "Hey everyone, God is here in Christ, reconciling the world to Himself, not counting against us our trespasses, but nailing them to this cross." It was only through the lens of Easter that such an understanding came. There are very few difficult, travailing experiences in your life that make sense while you are walking through them.

The passage of Scripture found in Mark 11 comes in the heart of Holy Week, just a few days before the crucifixion. Jesus' practice was to spend each day in Jerusalem and then leave the city and spend the night with His friends in Bethany. Our passage begins with Jesus making His daily trip into Jerusalem. Just outside of Bethany, as He was making His way into the city, Jesus saw at a distance a fig tree in full leaf. Mark 11:12 says that Jesus was hungry, so He walked over to the fig tree to see if there was any fruit on the tree, but when He got there He found nothing but leaves. Interestingly, Mark records that it was not the season for figs. But Jesus cursed the fig tree and said, "May no one ever eat fruit from you again!" (v. 14). The disciples heard him say this.

Jesus entered the city, went inside the temple, and drove out those who were buying and selling. He overturned the tables of the money changers in an act of judgment against greedy religious enterprising. Jesus taught in the temple and then went home and spent the night in Bethany again.

The next morning Jesus got up and again made the trip into Jerusalem. But on the way out of Bethany, the disciples saw the fig tree that Jesus had cursed the day before, and it was withered from the roots up, dead, lifeless. This is the same twenty-foot tree that a day earlier had been in full leaf! The disciples were amazed. Peter said to Jesus, "Rabbi, look! The fig tree you cursed has withered!" (v. 21). They realized that it was a miracle, a prophetic act by Jesus that meant something.

This fig-tree story is like a parable that is lived out or acted out. Jesus often told parables, stories from everyday life, using illustrations that were familiar to His listeners, like a farmer sowing seed, a fisherman catching fish, a merchant looking for pearls, a woman putting some yeast in dough, or shepherds looking for a lost sheep. These are all everyday scenes from life that illustrate some point about the kingdom of God. This event is like that, except that it was not a story Jesus told, but a story He acted out.

If you are familiar with the Old Testament, you may recall that the fig tree is mentioned more than forty times in Scripture. It has come to represent Israel in much the same way that the bald eagle represents the United States. The Bible often uses the fig tree as a symbol or metaphor for Israel. As the fig tree goes, so goes the nation. First Kings 4:25 characterizes Israel during the height of their prosperity by saying,

"During Solomon's lifetime Judah and Israel . . . lived in safety, each man under his own vine and fig tree." The fig tree symbolizes Israel in prosperity and under God's blessing. On the other hand, in Jeremiah 8:13, when the people refused to repent and return to the Lord, the prophet said that God will judge the people and "there will be no figs on the tree." The prophet was not merely predicting a crop failure. He was picturing Israel under judgment. This is a familiar feature of ancient writings. Israel was going to wither and die, and that fact was symbolized by the barren fig tree.

In Micah 4, when the prophet presented the final restoration, the consummation of the ages, a glimpse into the new creation, he declared, "They will beat their swords into plowshares and their spears into pruning hooks. Nation will not take up sword against nation, nor will they train for war anymore. Every man will sit under his own vine and under his own fig tree" (vv. 3–4).

Later in Mark's gospel, Jesus would again use the fig tree as a symbol of Israel (see Mark 13:28–30).

He also used the fig tree as a symbol in Luke's gospel, where he told the story of a man who had a fig tree planted in his vineyard. He later came to that tree looking for fruit but found none. The second and even the third year, he still found no fruit. Finally, he went to the landowner. "For three years now I've come looking for fruit and found none," he said. "Should I cut it down?" The master replied, "No, leave it alone for one more year. I'll dig around it and fertilize it. If it bears fruit, fine. If not, then cut it down" (Luke 13:6–9, paraphrased). The fig tree was symbolic of the nation of Israel. Year after year they had rejected the Messiah in their midst. They were disobedient and rebellious, and now the time of judgment had come. However, God, in His mercy, extended to Israel a final window of grace.

So, in light of the figurative importance of the fig tree, the cursing of the fig tree in Mark 11 was a highly significant prophetic action. In Palestine, the fig trees show their leaves in March, and by April they are in full foliage. They don't bear ripened figs until

June, a full six weeks after the time Jesus saw this tree, which is why Mark pointed out that it was not the season for figs. But as with all fruit trees, the forerunner of a fully ripened fruit is a fruit knob of some kind, and in the case of fig trees, it is already edible, what we would call a "green fig." The poor often ate these little knobs. But if the forerunner of the fruit is absent, it means that the tree is barren. If by April the tree does not have anything, it is not going to bear fruit six weeks later. However, the tree that Jesus cursed did not give the appearance of a dead, barren tree; it was in full foliage. He fully expected to see a fruitful tree. When He approached it and saw that it was barren, despite having the appearance of fruitfulness, it was an irresistible parable waiting to be lived out. To be visibly barren is one thing, but to have the appearance, the outward show, of fruitfulness and yet, upon close examination, have no fruit created an apt opportunity to make a powerful statement about Israel—that they were outwardly impressive but inwardly barren.

Israel was, like this fig tree, all show but no substance. At Passover, Israel was in the midst of one of the most impressive religious displays imaginable. It showed so many signs of fruitfulness: the temple, the crowds, the phylacteries, the menorahs, the fancy candles, the gilded altars. It was all so outwardly impressive, but upon close examination, our Lord found it to be barren and fruitless. Lots of leaves, but no fruit. Despite its ambitious boasting, but when examined by our Lord, the nation was found to be empty, false, and hollow. Israel was at the height of her national glory. It had taken the nation forty-six years to build their glorious temple. It was one of the wonders of the world. However, it was in the midst of these pursuits that they rejected and crucified their Savior, Lord, and Messiah, Jesus Christ.

This story about Israel is, of course, not just a story about their rejection of Jesus Christ even in the midst of all their religiosity. It is a parable for us all. One cannot help but notice the decline in the emphasis on repentance and the lack of spiritual reflection that happens in our own churches, even as we build big programs and even bigger structures. This passage calls us all to a time of spiritual scrutiny. We should not accept a church where celebration overtakes confession. We should not embrace a "grab-a-cup-of-coffee-and-make-yourself-comfortable" approach to worship. We can become quite good at growing a lot of leaves, but not having much fruit, at creating outward religious displays, while ignoring the deep fruitfulness that the Lord is looking for in our lives.

Jesus Christ is drawing near to all of us for a close examination. When He does, will He find fruit, or just a lot of leaves?

Seven

God Writes Straight with Crooked Lines

2 Corinthians 2:12–17

Have you ever wondered if you are really living in God's will and doing what He wants you to do? Sometimes it is very difficult to see God's will when you are walking through it. Life seems crooked, erratic, and even out of control. We don't always see His hand, feel His presence, or know if we are hearing His voice. Perhaps a lesson from the life of the apostle Paul might be encouraging to you.

A paradox is not a contradiction; it is an apparent contradiction. In this chapter's passage we find three paradoxes in Paul's life.

The first one we encounter is the paradox of God's timing. Paul wrote, "Now when I went to Troas to preach the gospel of Christ and found that the Lord had opened a door for me, I still had no peace of mind, because I did not find my brother Titus there. So I said good-bye to them and went on to Macedonia" (2 Cor. 2:12–13).

Troas was a very strategic place to preach the gospel. As the chief point of northwest Asia Minor, it was a major commercial, athletic, and intellectual hub and would have been a suitable base for missionary activity. Troas was also an important meeting point—a natural place of rendezvous. There, Paul had expected to meet Titus, who had been sent from Ephesus to Corinth, and an unnamed companion as the bearer of the letter we know now of as First Corinthians. Paul arrived there and found an open door of opportunity, but he had no relief in his spirit. Have you ever felt that way? Paul did not know what to do. He wanted to go into Asia Minor, but the Holy Spirit kept prompting him to not go there. Finally, one night, Paul received a vision of a "man of Macedonia," who pleaded with him to come over to Europe (Acts 16:6–10). Paul determined that this must be the call of God, so he crossed over into Europe and had a very fruitful ministry. This is where he encountered Lydia, the cloth dyer, who became the first European to turn to Jesus Christ. This would be the door that would lead to major church plants in Philippi, Thessalonica, Athens, and Corinth.

Years later, Paul was on his third major missionary journey and had no intention of going to Troas. He went instead to Ephesus and spent more than two years there and traveled to other parts of Europe. Finally, he made arrangements to return to Syria and Jerusalem. However, in Acts 20:3 we are told that Paul discovered a plot against his life, and at the last minute he decided to not return by ship, but to travel by land. This brought him, quite unexpectedly, to the city of Troas, where he had a great ministry.

Have you ever felt God calling you to do something, and then it all seemed to go awry, only to find years later how it all made sense? In the summer of 1990, I left six years of pastoral ministry to work in Nigeria. However, we encountered numerous obstacles and finally were forced to abandon our plans and not move to Nigeria as we had planned. It was a difficult time for us as a family. When I returned to the United States from Nigeria, all my plans (which had seemed to be confirmed by God in so many ways) were in tatters. I recall telling my wife, Julie, "If God would just give me an explanation as to why we went through all of this, I could accept it." My wife wisely responded, "God doesn't owe us any explanations. Our job is to just be faithful and follow Him as best we can."

I ended up becoming the pastor of a small church in Carnesville, Georgia. That church was quite close to Toccoa Falls College, where I began to teach and, eventually, had a full-time career in teaching. Looking back, I can see how God used the whole experience to teach me to trust Him. There is an old Portuguese saying, "God writes straight with crooked lines." How true that is. I couldn't see what He was doing until years later.

In life, we, like the apostle Paul, do not always see God's will when we are walking through it. Sometimes, even major setbacks are but preludes to God's deeper work. All I saw was my circumstances and the limited vision of the year I was in this directional agony. God saw the whole canvas, and I was always right where He wanted me to be.

The second major paradox Paul encountered is found in verse 14 of our passage. Paul said, "Thanks be to God, who always leads us in triumphal procession in Christ." Another translation says, "But thanks be to God, who in Christ always leads us in triumph" (RSV). Paul was trying to be faithful to God and to the gospel. But as he outlined in 2 Corinthians 11:24–29, at every turn he faced persecution. He was imprisoned, flogged, and exposed to death again and again. Five times he received from the Jews the forty lashes minus one. Three times he was beaten with rods, stoned, and left for dead. Three times he was shipwrecked. One time he even spent a night and a day in the open sea. He faced dangers from rivers, bandits, his own countrymen, and Gentiles. Frequently, he was hungry, thirsty, exposed to cold, or without adequate clothing.

Every outward measurement suggests that Paul was not experiencing the blessings of God. In fact, it must have felt as if God was abandoning him. But God writes straight with crooked lines. Paul was learning an important lesson about the relationship between our outward experiences and the blessing of God. You may not have experienced these kind of physical hardships, but you may have gone through a very difficult period where you just felt as though God had forsaken you. Paul recognized what we must also recognize: namely, that our victory is not based on outward circumstances. Titus would eventually reunite with Paul. Corinth would eventually reject the false teachers who had infiltrated their ranks. Paul would ultimately be known as the great apostle to the Gentiles. But none of that was the basis for his newfound confidence. Instead, Paul's confidence was found in the deeper truth that God always leads us. In his own words, "But thanks be to God, who always leads us as captives." It is the picture of a celebration of a military victory. In the ancient world, the captives would be paraded through the streets and exposed publicly. The word Paul used here means "to lead someone captive in a victory parade." Paul had once literally dragged Christians out of their homes and publicly disgraced and humiliated them. Paul who once captured others was now reflecting on his own captivity but of a different kind. Christ had, in effect, taken him captive through the power of the gospel. Though in this present life we may suffer and be exposed to the world's ridicule, by allowing ourselves to be captivated by Christ, we are able to share in His triumph!

We are servants of Christ. Only by becoming Christ's captives are we able to share in His triumph. He is leading a triumphal procession through the world. Paul affirmed the paradox: in Christ we are both conquered captives, slaves of Christ, exposed to the world's ridicule, and yet, at the same time, joyful participants in Christ's victory celebration! This is the paradox of the cross.

The third and final paradox Paul pointed to in this chapter's passage is found in verses 14–16, in which he drew upon the Jewish image of sacrifice. The sacrifice would fumigate the entire altar. Paul said that now we are God's sacrifice: "For we are to God the aroma of Christ among those who are being saved and those who are perishing." We are the aroma of Christ to the world—and that is the paradox. We are living sacrifices. The world sees us as the stench of death. We are those who are persecuted, shamed, and decried by the world. But God sees it not as the stench of death but the aroma of life. By any human standards—while he was in the midst of it—Paul's ministry was a disaster and a failure. Only by taking the long view and looking at it from a divine perspective could it be properly measured.

We often measure whether God is with us by the results and the world's standards of success. But God calls us to another level of faithfulness when things seem crooked and distorted and out of control. Our task is to live in *this* world but be judged by the standards of another world. It would be easy if we were called to live out our lives in some heavenly plane of existence, or if we were called to retreat from this world and live in a corner somewhere. But we have called to be His ambassadors right in the midst of a world who rejects our claims. We are called to take up our cross and follow Christ daily (Luke 9:23).

One of the most important passages to remember is that word of wisdom from Proverbs 3:5–6: "Trust in the LORD with all your heart and lean not on your own understanding; in all your ways acknowledge him, and he will make your paths straight."

God does make our paths straight, but He often does it through what seems like a lot of crooked lines. Truly, God writes straight with crooked lines.

Eight

The Suffering, Advancing Church

Matthew 11:12

Matthew 11:12 is not an easy verse to translate. Let me give two popular translations that seem to say two different things. The ESV translates Matthew 11:12 as, "From the days of John the Baptist until now the kingdom of heaven *has suffered violence*, and the violent take it by force" (emphasis added). In contrast, the NIV (1984) and the NLT (2015) translate it, "From the days of John the Baptist until now, the kingdom of heaven *has been forcefully advancing*, and forceful men lay hold of it" (emphasis added).

The text is clearly about the kingdom of God. The question is, what is being said about the kingdom of God? Is the kingdom of heaven suffering violence under the hands of those who wish to destroy it, or is it forcefully advancing, extending the claims of Christ's lordship into a lost world?

The word the ESV translates "has suffered violence" and the NIV renders "has been forcefully advancing" is the single Greek word *biazetai*. This word can be equally translated in passive voice, that is, what is being done *to* the church, or in active voice, what the church *is doing*. There is nothing in the word itself that leans one way or the other, which is why the translations come down differently. The context must make it clear. But even this is not easy.

To state the question clearly: Is this passage teaching that the story of the church of Jesus Christ is one of glorious advance into the world, or it is the story of a church under persecution, defensively holding on until Jesus returns to turn back the tide and defeat the onslaught of the world, the flesh, and the devil? Are we "suffering violence" or are we "force-fully advancing"? This is a very important question, because it serves to set our expectations about the role of the church in the world.

Interestingly, a similar tension is found in Matthew 16, where Jesus asked His disciples, "Who do people say the Son of Man is?" (v. 13). Peter famously replied, "You are the Christ, the Son of the living God" (v. 16). Jesus called Peter blessed and in verse 18 said, "And I tell you that you are Peter, and on this rock I will build my church, and the gates of Hades will not overcome it." The tension comes in the translation of the latter part of Jesus' response. Where Jesus said of the church, "the gates of Hades will not overcome it," it can equally be translated "the gates of Hades will not prove stronger than it" (NIV 1984, marginal notes). There are two different ideas here. Are the "gates of Hades" a metaphor for the powers of hell attacking the church, and the church prevailing even against the onslaught of hell itself? Or, is it the church of Jesus Christ that is forcefully advancing against the gates of hell, and the gates of hell cannot withstand the onslaught of the church as it vehemently advances Christ's claims in the world? It is the same tension. Is the church suffering violence or forcefully advancing? Is the story of the church the story of the advancing powers of hell not overcoming the church, or is it the story of the powerful advance of the church, which prevails against the very gates of hell itself?

This tension occurs a third time in Matthew's gospel, but this time in a different way. In chapter 24, Jesus' disciples were questioning Him about the end of time. "What will be the sign of your coming and of the end of the age?" they asked (v. 3). Jesus responded by reciting a long litany of terrible things that will happen to the church, describing the onslaught of the enemy in graphic detail. The church in Matthew 24:4–13 is a picture of a church "suffering violence." There will be wars and rumors of wars, nation rising up against nation, kingdom against kingdom. There will be famines and earthquakes in various places. Then, we are told that we will be handed over to be persecuted and put to death, and we will be hated by all nations because of Christ. Jesus went on to say that many will turn away from the faith and will betray and hate one another, and false prophets will appear and deceive many people. There will be an increase in wickedness, and the love of most will grow cold. This is a picture of a church that is holding on against the advancing powers of hell. Indeed, in verse 13 Jesus concluded His recounting of the church's end-time sufferings with, "But he who stands firm to the end will be saved." We are exhorted to be faithful, to persevere, and to await the coming of Christ.

However, the next verse is the most remarkable in the whole passage, especially when read in the context of Jesus' litany of the world's advances against the church, such as persecutions, martyrdom, apostasy, and so forth. Suddenly, like a light bursting forth into a dark room, Jesus said in verse 14, "And this gospel of the kingdom shall be preached in the whole world as a testimony to all nations, and then the end will come."

Jesus was saying that even though the world and all the hosts of satanic wickedness are advancing most forcefully against the church, and the church is seemingly on the defensive and just barely hanging on for dear life—*God* is triumphing. At the very moment the hosts of darkness launch their most powerful assault and God's kingdom seems to be suffering the worst violence the world has to offer, the Lord will make His move, overturning His foes and demonstrating the prevailing power of the gospel. This gospel of the kingdom shall be preached in the whole world as a testimony to all nations!

Perhaps we shouldn't be so surprised at this. After all, isn't this what God did at Calvary? As the beautiful Easter hymn declares, "The powers of death have done their worst, but Christ their legions hath dispersed."[6] As Jesus hung on the old, rugged cross,

---

6. "The Strife Is O'er, the Battle Done," *The United Methodist Hymnal* (Nashville: United Methodist Publishing House, 1989), no. 306.

the powers of death had done their worst. Darkness, it seemed, had prevailed. The Son of God, God's gracious gift to the world, had been cruelly executed. Who would believe that at that very moment, when it seemed as if darkness had triumphed and the powers of hell had secured their victory, a great light was bursting forth onto the world? Our greatest act of rejecting God became simultaneously His warmest embrace of us. Our worst hour, when we nailed God to a cross, became His finest hour, when He nailed our sins there. The ugliest, darkest, most revolting form of execution was crucifixion, and the cross itself was a symbol of hate and torture. Yet, that same instrument of torture became the greatest symbol of love and light. You see, this is the way God is. Death itself is swallowed up in His victory. How much more so all the other, lesser trials of life? The last few words the world ever said of Jesus were spoken in smug triumphalism: "He saved others, but he can't save himself," they mocked (Matt. 27:42; Mark 15:31). But never forget that it is God who has the last word.

Three days after the crucifixion, an angel announced on resurrection morning, "He is not here; he has risen" (Matt. 28:6; Luke 24:6)! God's purposes prevail, even in the face of the worst this world has to offer.

God faces that which is worst in us and transforms it into a testimony of His grace. The apostle Paul called himself "the worst" of sinners (1 Tim. 1:15), but by God's grace he, of all people, became the greatest of God's apostles. In reckless defiance of Christ, he had set out for Damascus to vent his hatred against the church of Jesus Christ. Yet, it was on that very road that God met him and said, "I will show you how much you must suffer for My sake, as you forcefully advance the gospel" (Acts 9:16, paraphrased).

We live in an age of ever-encroaching spiritual darkness, secular humanism, and postmodern cynicism, all of which shroud our lives like a deep fog. The church is suffering violence at every turn. We wonder sometimes if we can prevail against the onslaught of evil. Yet even amid this tumultuous and war-ridden world, we need to know that God is unfolding His plan.

Before the morning of June 6, 1944, known as D-Day, it appeared by all reckoning that Adolf Hitler would be triumphant in the global war that had been raging since 1939. He seemed invincible as his powerful armies swept through Europe. Hitler was drinking champagne in Paris as German bombs fell on London. But beneath the early morning fog of June 6, something else was under way. While Hitler was off celebrating his birthday, the Allies were quietly launching the decisive attack. Likewise, beneath the fog of this world, while many are unaware of God's unfolding work in the world, the gospel of the kingdom is being preached and sent forth to all nations in a way unprecedented in the history of the church.

In 1949, there were only about a million Christians in China. Since that time the Chinese church has experienced unparalleled persecution as the forces of evil set their face against it. But today, there are more than 75 million Christians in China. I was teaching in China during the summer of 1993 when I had the privilege, along with my colleagues, not only to lead several new Chinese to Christ and to baptize one in the Yangtzee River, but to meet many Christians who are willing to give their lives to extend the message of Christ into China. And they are spreading the gospel, even in the midst of growing darkness, right in the teeth of government hostility.

In India, beginning in the 1970s, the Indian government refused to grant new visas to support traditional Western missionary work. The number of foreign gospel workers has dropped from more than twelve thousand to fewer than two hundred today. But for every missionary that was forced to leave India, God has raised up not one, but two Indians who have given themselves full-time to expanding God's kingdom by bringing the gospel to the unreached peoples of India. For thirty years I have been closely involved in the spread of the gospel in India. There are thousands and thousands of new churches being planted all over this subcontinent, many among people groups who have never had a church, or any Christian witness, throughout history.

Across the great continent of Africa, the church is growing. An estimated sixteen thousand men and women are coming to Christ every single day across the continent. The gospel's spread across Africa is one of the great unfolding chapters in the history of the church. One hundred years ago, the representative Christian would have been a forty-seven-year-old British man. Today, it is a twenty-seven-year-old Nigerian woman. In 1981, the white races of the world, who for centuries represented the heartlands of the Christian faith, became the minority. That is how quickly the church of Jesus Christ is growing in Africa. South America is also experiencing a tremendous growth of evangelism. Evangelicals during the last century in South America have grown from 69 million to more than half a billion.

Time does not permit me to tell you of the remarkable things God is doing all over the world. The point is this: the church of Jesus Christ is forcefully advancing, even while many grow cold in their love for Christ, fall away, and lose the faith.

So, we conclude this chapter asking, again, how should we translate the word *biazetai*? Is the kingdom of God forcefully advancing or is it suffering violence? What has become clear is that it is experiencing, and always has experienced, both. Indeed, the church advances only as it is willing to suffer violence. Our suffering purges and cleanses us. Our advance extends the rule and reign of Christ. That is why God gave us in the inspired text the word He did. It is one of the few Greek words that simultaneously highlights both aspects of the church's life in the world.

The question before all of us is, where are we in this great move of God in the world? Are we going to participate in this great advance of the gospel, which is silently slipping across the world beneath the fog of so much else that catches the world's attention? Are we as the people of God going to step out and fulfill the mission of God in our own time? May we all learn to accept the sufferings of Christ so that we, too, can fully participate in God's forceful advance into the world.

God's Yes in Jesus Christ

In 1834, the great poet Samuel Taylor Coleridge wrote a poem entitled *The Rime of the Ancient Mariner*. In the poem a ship is being followed by an albatross, a large Pacific seabird with a wingspan of up to twelve feet. In the ancient world, it was widely regarded as a good omen for a ship to be followed by an albatross. However, in Coleridge's classic poem, one of the sailors shoots the albatross with a crossbow and kills it, bringing sure doom to the voyage. To allay the curse, the sailor who shot the bird is forced to wear the dead albatross around his neck. This is where we get the common saying that someone is bearing his burden "like an albatross around his neck."

It is a helpful image because sometimes we fall into the trap of thinking that God has laid an albatross around our necks. He is somehow against us, forcing us to carry a huge burden of guilt. Perhaps we have a mental picture of an angry God who is just waiting for us to slip up so He can say, "Gotcha." We often live under a cloud of internal condemnation and carry the weight of guilt and fear like an albatross around our necks. However, the apostle Paul reminds us in 2 Corinthians 1:20 that all the promises of God are "Yes" in Jesus Christ. God is for us. Brothers and sisters, God is for you! He stands with you this day, and His word for you is always *yes*.

You may ask, "What about all the times when God (or His Word) says no to us?" Well, when God says no, we must always listen carefully for the hidden yes behind it. Much of what we want God to say yes to are things that will bring isolation and destruction to us. So God says no. But He only says no because He is standing with us and longs for our deepest joy in fellowship with Him and others. God does not say no to crush our joy. He says no so He can say yes to our greater joy.

Perhaps you feel as if you have shot the albatross in your life. You have killed the very thing that was to bring you a blessing, and now you must bear that guilt and carry that shame for the rest of your life. But, today, hear the yes of God in Jesus Christ. This is the shared theme that ties all of the meditations together in this book: God's yes. In Jesus Christ, every sin has been paid for; every closed door flung wide open; every empty table filled with His abundance; every grave prepared for resurrection; every demon cast into the swine and sent over the hill. Every broken wall has been rebuilt; every crushed dream has been renewed; every crooked way has been made straight, the word of forgiveness always ringing louder than the word of guilt; every sunset of despair has been turned into a sunrise of hope! It is true that we do not yet see all of this. We still await the final consummation. But in Jesus Christ it is already breaking in! Satan is being crushed under our feet. The joy of the gospel is breaking upon us. The dead albatross is arising from our necks and taking flight to, once again, bring a blessing, not a curse. Today, may you hear afresh the Yes! of God in Jesus Christ.